BABY PENGUIN

Text copyright © 2001 by Aubrey Lang
Photography copyright © 2001 by Wayne Lynch

Published in Canada by Fitzhenry & Whiteside, 195 Allstate Parkway, Markham, Ontario L3R 4T8
Published in the United States by Fitzhenry & Whiteside, 121 Harvard Avenue, Suite 2, Allston, Massachusetts 02134

Printed in Canada by Goody Color Inc.

10 9 8 7 6 5 4 3 2 1

National Library of Canada Cataloguing in Publication Data

Lang, Aubrey
Baby Penguin

(Nature babies)
ISBN 1-55041-675-8

1. Penguins—Infancy—Juvenile literature. I. Lynch, Wayne II. Title.
III. Series: Lang, Aubrey Nature babies.

QL696.S473L35 2001   j598.47   C2001-901081-8

U.S. Cataloging-in-Publication Data
Library of Congress Standards

Lang, Aubrey.
Baby penguin / text by Audrey Lang ; photography by Wayne Lynch. –1st ed.
[32] p. : col. photos. ;   cm.   – (Nature babies)
Note: includes "Did you know" fact list.
Summary: The story of growing King penguin chicks and their life in the colony.
IBSN 1-55041-675-8 pb edition   IBSN 1-55041-670-7 bound edition
1. Penguins -- Juvenile literature. [1. Penguins.] I. Lynch, Wayne, 1948- . II. Title. III. Series.
598.47 [E] 21   2001 AC CIP

Fitzhenry & Whiteside acknowledges with thanks the Canada Council for the Arts,
the Government of Canada through the Book Publishing Industry Development Program (BPIDP),
and the Ontario Arts Council for their support of our publishing program.

Design by Wycliffe Smith

BABY PENGUIN

Text by Aubrey Lang
Photography by Wayne Lynch

Fitzhenry & Whiteside

BEFORE YOU BEGIN

Dear Reader,

We love to watch and photograph wild animals. Often they make us laugh; sometimes they make us cry. We wrote this book to share with you some of the exciting stories in the life of the king penguin, which most people will never see. We prefer to photograph animals in nature, not in zoos. And we take care never to harm our animal subjects or to interfere with them in any way.

The penguins in this book live on an island at the bottom of the world where the Southern Ocean meets the Atlantic. It was a long journey to get there. We sailed in a steel ship especially built to break through ice.

—Aubrey Lang and Wayne Lynch

4

TABLE OF CONTENTS

It is early summer at the bottom of the world, on an island near Antarctica. Even in summer the island of South Georgia is cold and windy—sometimes it snows.

Every year penguins swim to South Georgia to have their babies, and this year the beach is crowded with the colorful birds. Penguins—unlike most birds—cannot fly in the air, but they are experts at flying underwater.

These are king penguins—one of the largest species of penguin. The one-year-old chicks are fat and funny looking. They are fuzzy and brown, and as tall as kitchen tables. Their soft, fluffy feathers look like fur. When their parents are away fishing in the ocean, the chicks gather in large groups near the beach.

Pickup By: 5/4/2023

5233

BES

32090004532720

Baby penguin

King penguins live together in a crowded colony. Baby penguins whistle loudly when they are hungry. When the adults talk to each other, they sound like trumpets. When everybody talks at once, the colony is a very noisy place.

The colony is also a smelly, messy place. Penguins defecate everywhere, and the ground is covered with stinky, gooey mud.

Adult king penguins, their bellies bulging with fish and squid, return from the ocean every three or four days to feed their hungry chicks. The penguins usually travel in groups to protect themselves from the dangerous seals and killer whales that often wait for them close to shore.

With so many chicks that look alike, how do parents find their own baby in a crowd? They listen. Each chick whistles a slightly different tune, and penguin parents recognize their young. Even when other chicks beg for food, the parents will only feed their own baby.

King penguins have very small families—only one chick at a time. Both parents return from the sea at different times to feed their chick. The baby soon gets round and pudgy. After a large meal of slimy fish, the chick is usually stuffed. It falls asleep quickly.

Sometimes, on a sunny day, a chick's thick coat of feathers can be too warm. The young penguins try to cool off by panting. If that doesn't work, they fall on their bellies and lie flat on the ground with their flippers and feet stretched out. Then the ocean breezes can reach their feet and cool them off.

Big, fat elephant seals often live on the same beaches as penguins. Sometimes these blubbery beasts bulldoze through the middle of a penguin colony, looking for a place to sleep. The seals don't care about the others—they will crush any penguin that gets in their way. The crowded colony is forced to make room for these bullies.

As the brown chicks grow, they get braver and more curious. Now is the time to wander and explore. This young male chick is lost in the tall grasses along the colony's edge. After an hour of searching, the tired male finally discovers a path, but it leads him to a new and unfamiliar part of the colony.

There are only adult penguins in this section of the colony. Many of the adults have a big white egg balanced on top of their feet. They keep the egg warm by covering it with their fat belly roll. A penguin with an egg is very unfriendly. When the curious youngster gets too close, a grumpy adult pecks him, driving the chick away.

The penguin chick hasn't seen his parents for seven days now, and he is getting very hungry. The youngster sees an adult by the water and, thinking he's found his mother, begs her for food. But the stranger slaps him with a stiff flipper and gives him a painful peck.

The chick does not know it yet, but his parents will never come back. It's time for the young penguin to live on his own.

The lonely chick still hopes his parents will come home and feed him. As he waits at the water's edge, a big wave knocks him into the surf. The young penguin has never been in the water before, and he's frightened. Cold and soggy, he waddles back to the colony where there are other chicks his own age.

Now that the chick is on his own, he must exercise his flippers. Throughout the day he runs in circles, rapidly flapping his flippers until he gets tired. Exercise will build the strong muscles he needs to dive underwater and catch his own food. The hungry young penguin is anxious to leave the colony. But he's not quite ready.

Before he goes, the penguin chick must molt his brown baby feathers and replace them with shiny new adult feathers. A molting chick is a funny looking bird—he appears to have an adult body, but his head still looks like a baby's.

When the brave, young king penguin finally leaves the colony, he will wander at sea. He won't return until the following summer.

DID YOU KNOW?

- There are seventeen different kinds of penguins in the world. The largest is the emperor; the king penguin is the second largest.

- Only two penguins, the emperor and the adelie, spend their whole lives in Antarctica. Small islands south of New Zealand are home to the greatest variety of penguins—nine different species in all.

- The king penguin chick is slower to mature than any known bird—it takes ten to thirteen months for it to grow up and live on its own.

- Every king penguin chick spends a winter on land before it fledges (grows its adult feathers). It may get nothing to eat for five months, and it will lose up to sixty-eight percent of its body weight. But the king penguin chick resists starvation better than any other warm-blooded creature on Earth.

- King penguins are one of the deepest diving birds in the world. They can reach depths of 1000 feet (305 meters), where the ocean is totally black.

- Adult female king penguins pick mates that are colorful and have deep voices. The bright colors indicate good health. A male with a deep voice is usually big and fat—a good hunter.

- Every year, an adult king penguin spends four to six weeks molting its entire plumage. During this time, the bird must stay on land without eating, and may lose half its body weight.

- An adult king penguin stands over three feet (nearly a meter) tall and can weigh thirty-three pounds (fifteen kilograms).

- Because they make a good-sized meal, king penguins have many predators, including killer whales, leopard seals, fur seals, and sea lions.

34

INDEX

BIOGRAPHIES

When Dr. Wayne Lynch met Aubrey Lang, he was an emergency doctor and she was a pediatric nurse. Five years after they were married, they left their jobs in medicine to work together as writers and wildlife photographers. For more than twenty years they have explored the great wilderness areas of the world — tropical rainforests, remote islands in the Arctic and Antarctic, deserts, mountains, and African grasslands.

Dr. Lynch is a popular guest lecturer and an award-winning science writer.

He is the author of more than a dozen titles for adults and children. He is also a Fellow of the internationally recognized Explorers Club, and an elected Fellow of the prestigious Arctic Institute of North America.

Ms. Lang is the author of nine nature books for children. She loves to share her wildlife experiences with young readers, and has more stories to tell in the Nature Baby Series.

The couple's impressive photo credits include thousands of images published in over two dozen countries.